Lasting Lines….. a collection of memories from my early years plus several more besides, written in narrative, poetry and prose with a sprinkling of thoughts, words and quotes. A legacy for my children, grandchildren and future generations.

An everyday story of an island girl whose early days endured harrowing floods, school bullying and tears, yet they were definitely outweighed with much fun and laughter and silly mishaps too.

My bucket list has been pretty much exhausted I'm pleased to say but something I've always dreamed of, is to write a book. Not a novel - I've not got enough imagination I'm afraid. So what better subject to write about than myself. I've enjoyed writing bits and bobs of poetry for some years now and came up with the idea of my memoir written mostly in verse - Lasting Lines.

*You may say
I'm a dreamer
But I'm not
the only one*

John Lennon

LASTING LINES

Published by new Generation Publishing in 2023, Copyright © Patricia Marshall 2023

First Edition

The author asserts the moral right under the Copyright, Designs and Patent Act 1988 to be identified as the author of this work.

All rights reserved. No part of this publication may be reproduced, stored in a retrieval system or transmitted, in any form or by any means without the prior consent of the author, nor be otherwise circulated in any form of binding or cover other than that which it is published and without a similar condition being imposed on the subsequent purchaser.

ISBN
        Paperback 978-1-83563-041-9

www.newgeneration-publishing.com
New Generation Publishing

I DEDICATE MY BOOK OF MEMOIRS TO JOHN,
EMMA AND JONNY AS A LASTING LEGACY WITH
ALL MY LOVE

Contents

CHAPTER 1 - IN THE BEGINNING 7

CHAPTER 2 - THE FLOODS 13

CHAPTER 3 - HOME LIFE 19

CHAPTER 4 - STICKS AND STONES 34

CHAPTER 5 - LATER 40

CHAPTER 6 - A PIECE OF FAMILY HISTORY 52

CHAPTER 7 - A LITTLE ABOUT LONDON 63

CHAPTER 8 - TALES OF THE THAMES 67

CHAPTER 9 - THE YEAR OF 2020 79

CHAPTER 10 - LATTER YEARS 94

CHAPTER 1 - IN THE BEGINNING

Life as a child

Life, as a child on an island
Was without a doubt remote
Surrounded by water and sea shells
Salt marshes, seaweed and boats
Sandy beaches became our playground
With friends we'd spend all day
Picnicking, paddling and crabbing
In the rock pools along the way

Patricia.

I am Patricia
my name means
noblewoman
a patrician
it is my destiny
heart's desire
and personality
a name that signifies
freedom loving
and free spirited
I answer to Pat
Patty and Tish
amongst others!!

Where I'm from

I'm a child of the fifties
who lived on an island
along the Thames
surrounded by salt marshes,
seaweed and boats
where the annoying toll
of the lighthouse bell
rang every fifteen minutes
day and night.

I'm from the apples in our
orchard in the garden
where the chilly outside
lavatory stood with
squares of newspaper
hung from a hook.
I'm from unmade, clinker roads
where the coal-man delivered
his load of black,
dusty, smelly sacks.

I'm from the greenhouse,
humid and warm
where the sweet aroma of
tomatoes is still with me today.
I'm from hens running
around the garden
and freshly laid eggs
for breakfast.
I'm from the toasting fork
as I sat by the fire on winter
afternoons waiting
for my bread to toast

I'm from fishing rods and boats
and the smell of fish
and the gatherer of cockles
and mussels.
picnicking, playing and crabbing
on the beach, is where I'm from
where sandy, soggy sandwiches
were the norm
with a thermos flask of tea
I'm a child of the fifties
I'm from those memories
that's where I'm from

Where I grew up.

A Pebble dashed bungalow
Was where I grew up as a child
The area was like a shanty town
Many homesteads of a similar style

We had to bath in a tin tub
The lavatory was out the back
There was no central heating then
Just fires from coal in a sack

Winters were pretty awful
Especially when it was frosty
The windows iced up on the inside
And we had to scrape it with ferocity

There were no mods or cons back in the day
So mum did her best to adjust
She'd throw wet tea leaves on the carpet
And sweep it all up with the dust
Dad kept chickens and it has to be said
I didn't like them pecking me
But I loved picking up the day old chicks
In a box from the station in Benfleet

Our garden was a large one
With many flowers and hedges
Apples fell from the orchard of trees
And the greenhouse was full of veggies

The garden shed was full of tools
A lathe and much much more
Tucked away behind were outhouses
Which as kids we'd love to explore

My first school

My primary school was called Leigh Beck
A big white building with black iron gates
My reception class was around the back
Mrs Lording was my teacher's name

The first few days we played in the sandpit
As well as shops and lots of toys
There were plenty of things there to enjoy
For all of us girls and boys

After that of course we had to have lessons
Reading, writing and sums
Lastly chairs on desks and a goodnight prayer**
Before running out to our mums

****

**Jesus, tender shepherd hear me
Bless thy little lamb tonight
Through the darkness be thou near me,
Keep me safe 'til morning light

****

CHAPTER 2 - THE FLOODS

When I was 5 years old I endured the most scary night of my life. I still remember those horrifying events today, 70 years later as if it were yesterday.

It started off as a normal Saturday, being the last day of January 1953. After a busy afternoon helping daddy in the garden - feeding the chickens and pulling up weeds as well as getting mud up to our armpits, my sister Barbara and I were called indoors for our weekly bath in an old tin tub in front of the coal fire before going to bed. It was getting dark and a nifty breeze had whipped up outside. A few hours later we were still awake because the wind was now howling ferociously outside, the trees were swaying back and forth and most of the garden pots and paraphernalia were flying about everywhere. The noise coming from the iron garden gate furiously opening and closing with the force of the wind was very scary but mummy assured us everything was okay. So we went back to bed unaware of what dangers were looming.

I remember the sound of something or someone banging furiously on our back door and windows. Daddy immediately ran to the door and could see it was the old lady across the road dressed only in her night clothes, drenched in rainwater and very windswept. She was shouting and screaming "the sea wall has collapsed and the sea is coming down the road, get out, the sea is coming". This was 2am and thank goodness there was a full moon that night because the street lights were not working and I don't know how she found her way to ours, the water was swirling around her nightdress and getting deeper by the minute.

I remember mummy and daddy rushing around the house in a kind of mad panic stuffing clothes and things in a holdall of some kind. By now my sister Barbara aged 27 months old was awake and crying. There were no telephones in those days (well not for us) and I'm guessing that my parents literally had to sit tight in the hope that they would be saved.

We lived on an island you see, right at the farthest end at its narrowest point (in fact that area was known as "The Point") and the sea wall was literally about 500 yards from our house one way and about quarter of a mile the other way. We were simply between a rock and a hard place so to speak. The water had by now covered the garden completely and I can remember daddy going outside to fend for the chickens who were clucking about in confused terror, feathers flying everywhere. It didn't take long before the water was coming up the door step and into the house. There was lots of commotion and people calling out to each other, making sure everyone was alright. Some houses were worse off than others and many had people screaming and waving from upstairs windows and some from their roofs braving the elements.

Daddy's best friend Bert at school back in the 1930s lived next door to us in a house called the Anchorage. Anyway they were obviously in the same boat too - excuse the pun. The wind hadn't calmed down and the rain was gushing down the road. Around dawn we left through our back door and us girls were carried down the garden and lifted over the fence of our neighbours , Beryl and Bert where we joined a group of others from the road behind us. From somewhere there appeared to be a couple of dinghies waiting for us round by the front gate with soldiers. I imagine that they were sent to our part of the Island due to its vulnerability and it was now our turn to be saved, hence the delay in our leaving.

We were helped into a dinghy by some people and someone rowed us to the slightly higher ground of Park Lane. Most areas at this part of the Island had dykes alongside the roads, put in many years ago by the Dutch, ironically to take away any excess water. On our dinghy journey we passed an Army truck which had obviously overshot the road and had gone head first into the dyke and almost overturned and maybe the reason we had such a long wait for help. From there we walked along the flooded Point Road towards Maurice Road where an Army truck was waiting for us.

There I remember being literally hauled onto the back by the soldiers, not quite by the scruff of the neck like a cat but it felt like it. There I sat waiting with lots of others for mummy, daddy and Barbara to join me. It was cold and we were all very wet and somewhat bedraggled. People were all hugging their belongings and shivering, as we were. I could see through the the flapping canvas at the back of the truck the water was as black as ink. We were taken towards the town centre where we walked the flooded road to my grandparents bungalow in Lionel Road. I could never understand why we weren't taken straight off Canvey but of course my dad wanted to check on his own parents to see if they were safe. I believe they were in the throes of making their own evacuation arrangements but nevertheless they came with us on the next Army truck where we were picked up in Long Road.

We were then taken to the Benfleet Junior School in the High Road. How the truck was able to get over the bridge to the mainland I really don't know but I guess the tide may have gone down slightly by then. On arrival at the school we were given blankets and I remember someone offering my mum a small pile of dry clothing for us to change into and take with us - including vests and liberty bodices with rubber buttons on them. I can still remember that pile of clothes and thinking at that young age, how could we wear something that has already been worn by someone else. We were given hot drinks and food. Babies were given nappies and bottles of milk. I remember sitting on the floor up against the wall alongside lots of other mothers and children. We seemed to be there for hours.

Eventually we were able to make our way to Benfleet railway station where we boarded a train to Fenchurch Street and onwards to my other grandparents' flat in Middlesex. They had been worried, with no telephones in those days they were unaware of our imminent arrival. Living in such a small flat there was literally no room for us but we were put in touch with a work colleague of my nan called Laura in Brentford who was able to put us up for six weeks. I remember there was an older boy living there too and I was given a pair of his striped pyjamas to wear. I hated them and they had mother of pearl buttons - I haven't been able to bear to touch those buttons since. My dad did not come with us as be needed to stay behind to feed and look after the chickens!!

When we returned home again six weeks later it was to a very muddy and damp bungalow. The Council handed out carpets and blankets to householders. I also remember someone coming into school with some "goody bags" for all the children which contained things like soap, flannels, toothbrush and toothpaste and some little toys to play with. To this day I can still remember the smell of those goody bags.

I have feared water all my life and when it is very windy outside I still remember that dreadful night. It's only now that I've written this that I realise the acts of heroism of that night; the old lady probably saved our lives; the people who rescued us with a dinghy; the Soldiers who evacuated us in their trucks; the kind people of Benfleet who took us under their wing and donated those clothes, and of course my mum and dad whose first thoughts were to make sure us girls (and the chickens) were safe.

31st January 1953

It was January
it was windy,
it was wild
middle of the night
wet and cold
the wall no more
defends the sea
the water surged
with ferocity

The roads
flooded
houses too
scared people
climbing roofs
shouting, screaming
to be heard
to be rescued
to be saved

At dawn
our rescuers came
the army,
the police and
firefighters too
with words of comfort
and dinghies
for evacuation
from this flooded island
to the mainland
seven miles away

31 January 1953

Aged five years old with a sister of two
We didn't quite know what was wrong
It was dark and raining and windy too
We were frightened all night long

Mummy and Daddy said all was okay
But we'd have to leave straight away
On with our hats, coats and boots
We were carried into the foray

The water was rushing and gushing
All down the road with plenty of influx
It was very scary and we were crying
But the soldiers rowed us to their army truck

We were then hauled onto the back
Women and children went on first
We were wet and muddy, cold and alone
And finally daddy was let on at last

We were huddled together in the back of the truck
And people were crying in despair
I looked out of the back and all I could see
Was deep dark water everywhere

They evacuated us to a primary school
Over on the mainland across the bridge
Where we were handed dry clothing
Hot tea and milk for us kids

We were housed as evacuees in London
By an acquaintance of my gran
But daddy stayed with our chickens at home
We thought him a very brave man

CHAPTER 3 - HOME LIFE

Shelling peas.

Shelling peas on the doorstep,
When I was six years old
Was a regular chore on a Sunday
Before lunch in our household
Scrubbing new potatoes
And carrots for the pan,
Chopping fresh mint for the sauce
To serve with the roast leg of lamb

Swimming.

I learned to swim when I was young,
Weekly, to a nearby pool
We went by coach as it was just too far
From where I went to school
Now here's the thing I tried to swim
But I was scared and kept my feet on the ground
I improved my skills to earn a badge
And I didn't even drown!

Mum's perfume.

My mum's perfume when I was a child
In nineteen fifty four
Came in a bottle of navy blue
In her dressing table drawer
I loved the smell as she wafted by
When she went out during the year
All dressed up in fur coat and heels
With "Evening in Paris" behind her ears

Jumble sales

My mum used to drag us to jumble sales
And queue up for what seemed like hours
They were a bit like today's charity shops
Second hand clothes to be scoured

Once inside, normally the church hall
There was an almighty scramble
All the mums scuffling and grabbing
More clothes than they could possibly handle

Traipsing around whilst mum filled her bag
With stuff that we'd probably loathe
And we did, our faces said it all
We hated these secondhand clothes

Bread and Dripping

Roast dinner on Sunday was a real treat
Normally a chicken (from those outside)
But on occasions we'd have lamb or beef
With all the trimmings and more besides

Now here's the thing, the following day
Meat juices from the bottom of the pan
Had solidified, fat on top jelly underneath
And just like that we had Dripping

Bread and dripping was one of those things
That you would either love or hate
It was yummy and tasty it lasted all week
I loved it, but for more I'd have to wait

Sunday evening at the pub.

Back in the day on sunny weekends
They enjoyed a drink at the pub
Mum and dad went inside themselves
And left us together outside on our own

They'd pop out to check us every so often
Ensuring we were ok and still there
Bringing lemonade and packets of crisps
But It was ever so very unfair

I'm talking of the nineteen fifties here
When this was the norm everywhere
All our school mates 'experienced the same
But nowadays parents wouldn't dare!

Hospital

I was eight when I had my tonsils out
And stayed in hospital for a week
I'd never been away from the parents
I hated it and when they left I shrieked

I hated every single day and night
The nurses woke me up so early
Just so they could put that horrible
medicine down my neck very sternly

I seemed to wait hours and hours for
Visitors, it was usually mum or dad
One day they brought in lots of cards
Made by my classmates - the best day I'd had
And finally I was able to pack my bags
And leave to go home on the bus
I'd hated being homesick, lonely and the smells
but now you wouldn't see me for dust!

Don't like veggies

There's nothing worse than hating
Something on your plate
No matter how often I said no
It was always there lying in wait

Brussels sprouts were my problem
Didn't like the smell or taste
I'd often try to hide them
Under something on my plate

I even tried to feed the dog
But always got caught out
I had to sit at the table
Until I'd finished the lot

By now I was ready to regurgitate
And then I'd get sent to bed
And "you'll eat it for breakfast"
Or "you'll have dried bread"

"There's plenty of people who are starving"
They'd say, "just put it in and swallow"
I deigned to say "well send it to them then"
So you can imagine what followed…

I remember

I remember being 7 years old
enjoying making perfume
out of rose petals and water
with my friend Maureen
in her garden

learning
to ride my bike
A second hand one
painted red

the doll house
my dad built and the
fun I had playing with it

Rupert the
Bear books that my
Grandma kept at her house
for when we stayed there

running through
the garden sprinkler
on hot sunny days
shrieking with joy
with my sister Barbara

I remember happy
Christmases where the
tree festooned with fairy lights
sat in the bay window
and the wonderment
of Christmas Eve
and counting the hours
until bed time
magical

snowy winters
and having fun outside
making angels
in the snow
and snowmen
and snowballing

I remember it so well

Leaking time

Time has a way of leaking unnoticed
It's not forgiving, it runs away
when you least expect it
so hold on to it, don't let it stray

Boating.

From the age of nine or ten
Depending on the tide
Weekends were spent aboard our boat
Which I disliked, and cannot deny

We'd leave the mooring early morning
After sleeping aboard all night
Sleeping bags and Tilley lamps,
(Ugh, the fumes) which we disliked

Once we'd left the creek, we headed out
To what's called the Hadleigh Ray,
Sandbanks surrounded us for miles and miles
And the water stayed all day
At first it was fun and we'd dig and play
And walk to Leigh for some chips
The novelty wore off by the end of summer
As boredom kicked in and we dreaded more trips

Saturday mornings

Saturdays when we were kids
Were pretty much the same
We'd catch the bus to visit gran
And then go home again

Gran always made an apple pie
For after our Sunday lunch
Her pinny usually coated in flour
But we always had something to munch

Out in the garden was grandpa Pop
Tending his array of flowers
His veggie patch and greenhouse too
Was where he spent many happy hours

So, time to go home on that same old bus
Armed with all kinds of foodie treasures
Whilst there gran made a meat pie or two
And threw one in for good measure

Earnings

After school when I was nine
You'd find me hunting around
To look for empty Tizer bottles
The sweet shop paid 3d if found

All us kids were doing it
To earn our threepenny bits
We'd knock on doors and ask around
In case we might have missed

On Fridays we'd tot up our stash
Sweet shop here we come
Sherbet dippers, gobstoppers,
Penny chews and bubble gum

An adventure

I'll never forget the time when I was thirteen
A friend and I wanted an adventure
We rowed a dinghy out in the creek
And came to a dodgy ending

Moored nearby was a huge Catamaran
And we wanted to row under its hull
There was plenty of room as far as we knew
So we promptly began to scull

Alas it wasn't as easy as that
We got caught up with a rope with a kink
In our effort to untangle and make our way back
The dinghy sank and we ended up in the drink!

CHAPTER 4 - STICKS AND STONES

Sticks and stones

Sticks and stones
May break my Bones
But names will never hurt me
Not so - don't be fooled
Children can be so very cruel
I dreaded going to school
Their problem was my name - Bones
That was my downfall
I hated school

It hurt, really hurt

I had to pretend it was okay
Every single day
From age five to fifteen
From almost day one, it started
I was pushed from behind me
And landed on the desk in front
Which knocked out my two front teeth.

It hurt, really hurt

That was just the beginning
The name calling, the laughing
The avoidance of kids
Never making friends
Jokes, songs about Bones
It hurt, really hurt
And I was still in primary school.

Walking home from school was a testing time
Kids mocking me, cajoling me
It hurt, really hurt
It came to a head when kids surrounded me
And dared each other to do it
IT - being they slit my wrist for a laugh
I wasn't laughing

It hurt- really hurt

Secondary school was awful
The jibes, the jokes which really hurt
It didn't help that I was stick skinny
And that just made it worse

I'd avoid the perpetrators to my very best
I'd hide if I saw them coming
Dem bones, dry bones, skinny bones
I'd hear the songs they were humming

The trouble was, once they knew it hurt
The more they'd keep harassing me
My bags were emptied, coats hidden
The bullying never ceased

My schooling began to take a dive
I became the class clown
I played up in lessons day after day
I guess to earn friends who'd not put me down

I realise now, some sixty years later
I should have ignored it all
Should have taken a stance
But I didn't and I felt like a fool

The moral of this story is to never let them see
How very vulnerable you are
To walk away with your head held high
After all it's their problem not yours

Repercussions

Sadly I never told mum and dad
Of the bullying I endured at school each day
I kept it all to myself you see
In the hope it would all go away

By the time I was six I'd developed tics
A nervous reaction I now know
Mum took me to the doctor who laughed,
patted my head and said "it'll soon go"

Over the years my confidence drained
I was nervous and it really showed
I was always looking over my shoulder
For fear that I was being followed

Children can make such nasty remarks
Verbal abuse is vile and obscene
I'm sure there were kids worse off at school
But it was me who suffered, unseen

Over the years I cringed
Saying that Bones was my name at birth
I'd be embarrassed, unnerved and blushing,
Waiting and dreading their mirth

Bullying - it hurts you know.

It wasn't my fault.
I was only very young
When the bullying started
Only five years old.
It wasn't my fault
I didn't ask for my surname
And nobody had ever
Taken any notice before
The playground was
The worst place
The taunting, ignoring
They even shut me
In a coal hole
Hardly bigger than me
They locked the door
It was dark and I
Screamed to be let free
I couldn't breathe
I was scared
How dare they
I have been claustrophobic
Ever since that day
My tics were getting worse
Which didn't help
I still have them
It really wasn't fair
It wasn't my fault

Focus

Focus on the path in front of you
Keep going, you're allowed
Leave your fears behind you
Pause, Breathe and be proud

CHAPTER 5 - LATER

The day I started work was the day I fled my nest, so to speak. I was beginning a new life, new area, and around new people. Aged just fifteen I was at last able to be ever so slightly independent, even though I was still living at home but I wanted - no I needed to be respected by other people for once in my life.

I started work in the City of London and I was welcomed by my new colleagues, most of whom were either Mods or Rockers which was the culture, bikes and fashion trending at the time. I fitted in well and had no undue worries. We all got on well and spent many a lunch hour in the, then well known record shop Keith Prowse in Fenchurch Street listening to the latest vinyl songs in the charts in the soundproof record booths. Everyone was doing it. Rarely did anyone buy anything.

My dad had always been adamant that when I left school I was absolutely never to work in a factory or a shop! Now you have to realise that we're talking about the 1960s here when the only jobs a girl could do were things like hairdressing, telephonists, shops or offices. Unlike today where there are many opportunities for good solid careers such as doctors, lawyers, engineers, scientists, architects and teaching. Back then it was just a job that you'd stay until you found something that caught your eye.

My dad had never wanted me to take my GCEs and stay on at school like many of my peers were. Something in later life I resented. His reasoning being that a girl would be married one day and that it would be a waste of time. It suited me at the time but………

Life on an island.

Life, as a child on an island
Was without a doubt remote
Surrounded by water and sea shells
Salt marshes, seaweed and boats.
Sandy beaches became our playground
With friends we'd spend all day,
Picnicking , paddling and crabbing
In the rock pools along the way

Whichever way you travelled
The sea was always there
This island was not forgiving
But as kids we did not care
It really was a lonely place
For reasons only known to me
and I dreamt of one day escaping
Over the bridge across the creek

Joy of joys my schooldays over
My night school served me well
Many hours of typing practice
To the chords of William Tell
So off to the 'Smoke 'as the City was known
In search of a suitable vacancy
Pleased with myself and dressed for the part
I entered the Employment Agency

And so, my career was beginning
When a clerical job was secured
I started my post in July sixty two
Now a change in my life was assured
Delighted to be a commuter at last
I could brush off the memories I'd endured
As the doors of my childhood now opened
I could now leave the island behind

I was paid the sum of five pounds a week
For a clerical job not bad pay
Maureen and Doreen and Rita as well
All showed me the ropes day by day
My days were filled with learning the job
Filing and phones and manning the office
It didn't take long to master the work
And soon I was no longer a novice

Where I am from

I am from loving parents
Estella and Sidney Bones
with ancestors from France
and Wormingford, Essex

We moved from Harrow
to an island
along the Thames
when I was three years old
where my sister Barbara
was born and a new
playmate for me

I'm from Saturday morning
pictures at the local flea pit
where films like Laurel and Hardy
and westerns were shown
while eating bags of sweets

I'm from walks along
the sea wall
with the parents
stopping off at the
amusement arcade
to use up the pennies
weighing down my pockets
and eating a candy floss
or toffee apples
and getting very sticky

I'm from a life by the water
where boats of all
shapes and sizes
tempted dad to buy one

and join the yacht club,
where trips to the Boat Show
at Earls Court
were an annual must
I became a Sea Ranger
messing around with boats
and learning to paddle
A canoe

I am from "I don't care who started it"
"when I say no - I mean no"
"I'm not made of money"
"you'll get square eyes"
"turn that music down"

Reflections

I'm from a plethora of
Great aunts and uncles
on my paternal side
who visited at Christmas
in their droves
from their homes in London
where much piano and
singing and laughter took place
in my grandma's front room

I'm from a dad who was a gas man
and mum a dinner lady
who also did homework for a
local business man
painting toy soldiers or stuffing
envelopes with this and that
I'm from exciting times
when I was sixteen
and mum surprised us
with a new baby Sister
Helen
presented to us
in a bundle
on the new yellow table
in the kitchen.
So sweet and cuddly
but boy did she cry a lot
I mean a lot
Reflections of Happy days
is where I'm from

Youth club

In my young teens in the early sixties
There was nothing to do, nowhere to go
Except the school youth club on a Thursday night
They put on something called a "Disco"?

The fashion of the day was very full skirts
With a "can can" petticoat underneath
Layers of stiff netting, the bigger the better
Swishing and twirling for all to see

"The lion sleeps tonight" was a favourite tune
And the "Twist" was currently number one
Twisting and turning, bending and moving
Exhausting it was, but so much fun

Music

Music
is what feelings
look like
it calms my soul
evokes many memories
from my yesterdays

Saturday job.

I once had a Saturday job
When I was just fourteen
A ladies hairdressers in the town
To keep the salon clean
I swept the floor and dried the towels,
Scrubbed all the sinks and made the tea,
Washed the brushes and cleaned the combs
And answering the phone, was me

I was very worn out by the end of the day
But enjoyed it all the same
It was time now to get the bus home
I'll be back next Saturday again

Books

There was definitely a lack of books
In my childhood home,
I don't remember reading the
Books I have since known.
Why oh why I have to ask
Did I not have them like my peers
I believe I must have missed a lot
During my formative years

Happy ?

Was I happy as a child?
I'm sure I must have been
I don't think I was unhappy either
except when Mum left us
when I was 11
that was bad
lots of tears
mega problems indoors
it was an awful time
and very scary
we were sent to our aunt and uncle
to stay, six weeks in all
we came home
Mum had returned
and it was never, ever, ever
spoken about again
I was happy

Or was I?

Secrets

Secrets
She had many
Things overheard and guessed
Many years I had wondered, but...
They were hers

CHAPTER 6 - A PIECE OF FAMILY HISTORY

Family

A link to the past
and a bridge to our future
is our Family

Family history

Family history is more than a tree
It's tracing our ancestors' past
Where do I come from, who came before me
Are questions I wanted to ask

So some years ago with my notebook and pen
I spoke to relations who may help my task
The older the better, the grands and the greats
And I wasn't afraid to ask

Letters, old photos and dare I say
Snippets of gossip or secrets divulged
They maybe correct or even embellished
But whatever, they are stories to be told

I gathered together as much as I could
I used census records to unearth
What their lives were like decades ago
Where they lived, occupation and birth

Another tool to look back in time
To discover the family in depth
Is the usefulness of certificates
Births, marriages and deaths

Once I'd cobbled together their story
And discovered about all that mystery
I was proud to pass on all that I'd gleaned
Linking past to the future - family history

Frances Smith

My great Granny Smith was London born
In eighteen seventy three
In Kensington workhouse I'm sad to say
For reasons then unknown to me

I did a spot of research and it came to light
She was born out of wedlock in poverty
Her mother was just 17 years old,
But the putative father, who was he?

She attended the local Ragged school
The family were very poor
I'm guessing this was a lasting secret
No one's mentioned it before

I was seven years old when I first saw her
In nineteen fifty four
It was near Christmas and snowing
As we approached her front door

She welcomed us on her doorstep
Polished and shining bright
She wore a crossover pinny
And her hair was very white

She took us to the front parlour
It was dark and we could not see
With curtains drawn and only used
on Sundays for visitors and afternoon tea

Such a sad start for Granny Smith
And her early years were not good
But she married Charlie and had ten children
And happy, after all she'd endured

Grandma Kate

My paternal gran from Notting Hill
Was a milkmaid when not very old
I guess she worked for the dairy
Or even a private household

She wore a yoke over her shoulders
To carry the heavy pails
Delivering milk to the neighbours
To help pay her family bills

In later years she became a cook
In a company called GEC
After retiring her baking was great
And we loved her apple pie for our tea

My French connection.

My maternal grandma Alice was born in 1899
Valenciennes was where she lived
Her parents owned the Boulangerie
And baked for all the village

She met my grandpa William during WW1
Who was with the Royal Engineers
As a despatch rider they must have met
When on his way back from the frontier

When the war was over they courted for a while
And they married in September '22
They packed their bags and off they went
To England and pastures new

Before me

Mum and Dad were born in London
in 1925 and '20 respectively
They met after the WW2 in 1946
When they both worked at the GEC

Dad had served in North Africa
With the Royal Engineers
Maintaining the armoured tanks
And was out there for several years

Mum applied to become a Land Girl
But alas it wasn't to be
She made aircraft radar equipment
A reserved occupation you see
Instead she did holiday work on a farm
Driving a tractor and digging up spuds
She also joined the ambulance corps
As an attendant, which she loved

After the war was over dad stayed on for a while
The army took him to places he'd never have known
It gave him a chance of discovering
Tunisia, Sicily, Naples and Rome

So, on home ground the two of them met
He was engaged to another and so was she
But they eventually married in September that year
And the rest is history…..

Dad's military service

Dad never spoke about the war and all I knew was that he served in Tunisia. It was very hot and the sand got everywhere and so did the flies. He had also mentioned Sicily and Italy and I remember seeing some photos once. Other than that I didn't have a clue.

About twenty years ago I wrote to the Ministry of Defence to enquire if they had anything on their records that might be of interest to me. I was delighted to receive a potted history of his service career. It was the best £20 I have ever spent as the information gave me lots to go on in my endeavour to see what he had been doing.

As a skilled engineer working with the GEC dad joined the Territorial Army in 1938 prior to the war breaking out in September 1939. It was from the TA that he joined the regular army. After initial training and going through the ranks he was eventually made up to Sergeant and posted to the newly formed Inspectorate in the REME - Royal Electrical Mechanical Engineers, where he was in charge of and oversaw the maintenance and day to day running of the tanks and other armoured vehicles.

He was posted to Tunisia on 8th November 1942. His unit was attached to the Eighth Army and after the the Tunisian campaign was over on 12th May 1943 they went on to capture Sicily and by late 1944 the army group pushed northward through Italy, capturing Rome which was finally defeated in Spring 1945.

This little potted history on two pages of A4 was enough to start many years of research into dad's service. It listed the medals he had won, physical description on enlistment and details of his family. His testimonial read.

"An extremely good tradesman, selected for Inspectorate duties. Sober, reliable and conscientious with a very pleasant disposition"

How proud am I !?

Grandpa Pop

Grandpa Pop was from Essex stock
Born in London in 1901
His name was Edward Buller Bones
And he lived in Kensington

In 1914 The Great War had begun
The men were all going off to fight
He was too young to sign up then
But a year later he joined, on a lie
Off he went to battle in Northern France
aged only fourteen years old
pretending to be his brother, he arrived
and it wasn't long before he was caught

So he came back to good old Blighty
Hanging his head in shame
His dad gave him a good ticking off
But you've got to admire his heroic aim

Family tree

It's not the size of the tree that
matters, It's the quality of the leaves
you find on there!

Blessings

I count my blessings every morning
A roof over my head
Food on my table
A Loving family
I'm happy

CHAPTER 7 - A LITTLE ABOUT LONDON

When I left school – too many years ago to count, I started work in the City of London as a filing clerk. Not the most promising of jobs I have to say but whilst I worked there I was busy having shorthand and typing lessons at evening classes so that I could 'improve myself' for future office and secretarial work.

This introduction to the City left me awestruck and I fell in love with it immediately. I have a passion for London but my overriding love is for the City and its history. I love the old buildings - The Mansion House, The Bank of England, The Royal Exchange and many more. My office was in Lime Street where I worked in the then 'Old Lloyds Building' which has since been demolished for the newer and more futuristic Lloyds Building designed by the architect Richard Rogers.

In later years I met my husband John who worked in marine insurance connected to Lloyds in the City. The after office life in the City in the late sixties was second to none and it was just by chance we were both in a pub called the New Moon that particular night in March 1969. In future years both of our children followed in our footsteps and commuted to the City – our daughter was in marine insurance and our son an Underwriter at Lloyds – it's somehow in the blood.

Anyway I digress. We go to London often, normally for walks down random alleyways, where we'll find a plethora of churches tucked away from the hub of the city, as well as the many footpaths along the Thames. A stroll along the South Bank is another favourite, where we find The Clink Prison museum. The prison dates back to 1144 making it one of England's oldest and most notorious prisons. Then we pass the Globe Theatre and the Tate Modern which was originally The Tate & Lyle sugar factory. From here you can view the wonderful St Paul's Cathedral and the Monument or you can walk across the Millennium Bridge and walk along the Thames Path back to the Tower of London.

My City

Suited and booted
I alight the train
A rush to the office
Walking through alleys
And many a lane
Passing churches
Markets and bars
The traffic never ceases
Buses, taxis and cars
Hustle and bustle
I love it
My city

Baby Boomer

I'm a baby boomer
I'm a teenager of the
Swinging sixties
where fashion, music
and attitudes had changed
in post war Britain
where Mary Quant and Twiggy
were household names
as was Vidal Sassoon
I loved the Beatles, The Who
And the Stones
It was cool to shop in
Carnaby Street and the Kings Road
London was the place to be
It was the party scene
Where Flower Power
And hippies abounded
Lucy in the Sky with Diamonds
Was a familiar tune
I never did drugs - ever
An era of wearing mini skirts
And long boots
Hot pants were all the rage
I'm from listening to Pirate radio ships
Radio Caroline comes to the fore
the Sixties were colourful and fun
And so so so much more……

That's who I am

CHAPTER 8 - TALES OF THE THAMES

I've lived in Essex since I was three years old and always by the coast. Canvey Island is a small island measuring approx 3 x 5 miles and sits just off the mainland in the Thames Estuary. Before it became the island it is today, during the first half of the century the only way onto the island was by means of stepping stones over the muddy creek when the tide was out or by a dinghy ferry when it was in. Now a bridge carries the heavy traffic onto and off the island.

From the age of about 7 or 8 years old, I spent many happy days playing in the sand and paddling in the rock pools on the beach at the top of my road with school friends - it was quite safe but I hasten to add something that would never occur these days, apart from anything else I couldn't even swim! Most weekends were spent on the Thames in my parents' boat off the coast of Leigh on Sea and Southend with several trips to the River Medway in Kent. I belonged to the Sea Rangers aged 14 and was always messing about on boats - canoes, dinghies, sailing boats - and I still couldn't swim!

As I said the river was just at the top of my road and just 800 yards off the foreshore was the Chapman Lighthouse on the Chapman Sands a series of mud flats which had been a problem for sailors and their vessels for hundreds of years.

The red iron framed structure rang a bell every fifteen seconds during foggy weather and believe me when I was a child, London and its environs suffered many "pea soupers" - a thick brown fog… I can tell you, and that darned bell would be ringing all through the night. Nowadays a bell bouy has replaced the old lighthouse which was demolished during the 1950s.

This area is known as "The Point" and takes you literally to the furthest point of the island from where you can see Leigh on Sea. Here beautiful purple sea heather grows in abundance and us girls took great pleasure in trying to pick some for mum. The aroma is still with me today.

The Thames

The Thames
From source to sea
Flowing, rushing, rolling
Under bridges, past palaces
Awesome

My corner of the world

The river Thames played a huge
part of my growing up
It was just at the end of our road
Where I'd play in the sand
Paddled in the pool
With friends
It was quite safe
(even though I couldn't swim)
Mum knew where to find me
And we always knew when
It was time to go home for tea
Even though we didn't have watches

Sundays by the Thames

As a family,
most Sunday afternoons
during the summer we'd be seen
walking along the sea wall,
watching all the boats cruising by
and fishermen catching their tea.
mum would pack up a picnic
and we'd walk over to the
salt marshes beyond the sea
wall when the tide was out -
being very mindful that the tide would
come in again within an hour or two -
very dangerous,
as we'd be cut off
from the mainland.

Salt marshes

Wandering across the salt marshes
When the tide had ebbed away
Jumping over the muddy pools
Where lashings of driftwood lay
Purple lavender, yellow heather
Very pleasing to my eye
Sounds of Curlews and rigging
On the sailboats high and dry

An angry sea.

We'd been sailing across the Thames
From its estuary to Chatham in Kent
But it soon became obvious
The weather was discontent.

The sea lashed out in anger
On that dark and stormy night
Our boat was rocking and rolling
And as kids we were sitting tight

The waves were crashing against the bow
The sails were almost down
The mast was rattling in the wind
And we wished we were homeward bound

Mum jumped onto the cabin top
To unravel the rigging and tackle
The wind was mean and the rain was sharp
And she held on in spite of her battle

We screamed at her to come on down
And at last she heard our cries
She'd managed to sort the tangled mess
And jumped onto the deck with pride

At last the angry sea calmed down
And we breathed a sigh of relief
The rain had stopped, the wind had dropped
We could now continue in peace

Old Leigh - Leigh on Sea

A small fishing village in the River Thames
Cobbled streets and seafood shacks
Muddy harbour and plenty of nets
Where fishing boats bring in their catch

The smell of landed fish in the air
And those gulls don't miss a chance
The noise they make and the way they glare
Their beaks are all ready to pounce

The fishermen's catch is not only fish
But cockles and mussels as well
Maybe a crab and a whimsical whelk
But they're all in the shack to sell.

A walk around the back of the sheds will find
Lots of boat paraphernalia
Lengths of gnarled ropes and rusty old chains
And old rotten boats that have seen better days

The charm of old Leigh is very unique
The sounds, the smells, the preys
And the walk along the waterfront
Where a rusty old anchor lays

Tower Bridge

Tower
Bridge raised for us.
When we sailed up the Thames
We were fooled, it was for the ship
Behind!

Motions of the sea

The Thames
rocking, rolling
yet sometimes calm and still
gently lapping on the shingle
it ebbs

The seashore

The breeze wraps itself around me
As I walk along the damp seashore
The gulls flying high, ducking and diving
The sand in my toes as I begin to explore

All kinds of shells, sea glass and pebbles
Were pleasing to my eye
Seaweed and rocks, driftwood too
And an odd crab scuttling by

I reach an inlet along the beach
I watch the rippling waves rolling in
The tide has turned, sand disappearing
I wonder what new surprises the sea will bring

The turning tide

As the tide turns
I feel the rush of hope at my feet,
The sea calms my emotions
As I watch the waves
And feel calmed by the
Sound as it flows away

Mud larking

All this was very new to me
I'd never heard of it before
The museum of London formed a group
Who led us to the Thames foreshore

Armed with wellies and rubber gloves
And a bag to collect our finds
We walked over pebbles and so much more
Mindful of the incoming tide

Our guide was more than helpful
With dating our finds and their histories
Of china, roof tiles and clay pipes
Which had lain in the Thames for centuries

Back breaking it certainly was
But it was fun to search for gems
A new experience and memories
Of time by our beautiful Thames

CHAPTER 9 - THE YEAR OF 2020

In the Beginning
February 2020:

In the beginning no hugs or kisses
Or shaking of hands or touch
Coughing and sneezing onto your arm
And hand washing was a definite must
Then Lockdown began and businesses closed
Social distancing now in place
Our Government insisting we stay at home
To ensure we are all keeping safe

Lockdown

March 23, 2020

Lockdown
Staying indoors
Keeping ourselves amused
Just wanting hugs from family
Miss them

Just saying

April 2020

Life's been taken for granted
And it's been going on for a while
It's taken this awful virus
To reflect on our lifestyle
Our pace of life was bustling
Chasing each day with great haste
Never taking the time to focus
On valuable time that went to waste

All this spare time we have on our hands
Give us the chance to reflect
On the value of life and our gratefulness
And things that we'd begun to neglect
The lawns have been cut, the cars are all clean
And the Do-it-yourselfers are there
The joggers, the cyclists and walkers too
Go out for their hour of fresh air

We're all so grateful to our NHS
Key-workers , front-liners and carers
Rainbows in windows to show our thanks
And clapping on Thursdays we all share in
Captain Tom has raised £31m pounds
By walking each day in his garden
In aid of our wonderful NHS
At a 100 years old we are heartened

We're learning how to make do and mend
And stretch our food much further
Jobs we thought we'd never get done
Are filling our time with great fervour
We're missing the hugs from our family

Thank goodness for FaceTime and Zoom
Let's hope we'll return to normality
Very Very soon

People are coming together now
And a community spirit abounds
As we count our blessings every day
A new look at life is profound
Let's now look forward to healthier times
And never will we ever cease
To remember those who sadly passed
May each one of them rest in peace

**STAY HOME - PROTECT THE NHS-
SAVE LIVES**

So awful

April 2020

Indoors
We're here to stay
Weeks of isolation
Means not seeing loved ones at all
Awful

In my garden

Today
Very mindful
Chaos all around us
Yet birds sing, flowers grow, sun shines
Surreal

Nature in lockdown

Cloudless clear blue skies
Birdsong breaking the silence
Heavenly solace

Easing
20th May 2020

Lockdown's slowly easing
And for many it's far too soon
It's been ten weeks for most of us
And it's very nearly June

My Journal of lockdown

June 2020

For years I've wanted to journal
And write down my thoughts each day
But I never seemed to find the time
And things just got in the way

But twelve weeks ago it seemed the right time
To pick up my pen and start jotting
To record my days, the routine and jobs
And how I'd get on with the shopping

I can't believe where the time has gone
The days and weeks have just flown
Busy with all sorts, clearing and sorting
Plus emails, texts and hours on the phone
Loads of new recipes and baking of cakes
Bread in the oven - just some of my tasks
Even my sewing machine came out to play
When I ventured to make us all masks

Good days and down days have all been noted
Lots of sadness, laughter and tears
As a wedding and birthdays are put on hold
And holidays cancelled until next year

So my journal is full and it's time to reflect
On the past twelve weeks we've endured
Never in my wildest dreams did I think
I'd need another journal - that's for sure!

Questions

July 2020

Was this all a wake up call
To teach us to be mindful
Grateful and kind?

Did it happen for a reason
So we could appreciate our friends
And families and lives?

What placed this plague among us
And shook the world we live in
With chaos, turmoil and strife?

Is the light at the end of the tunnel yet?
Will things go back to normal?
Or is this our "new normal" for life?

Easing?

August 2020

So August is here and lockdown's been eased
Too early, too much that's for sure
The beaches are crowded, the pubs just the same
Don't they realise the problems we'll endure

There's kind of a hint that guidelines may change
As travel restrictions are imposed
It's mandatory to wear a mask in the shops
But where this is going, who knows

The government assure us that lockdowns are local
But there's a definite rise in cases
Are we heading for further restrictions
As many worldwide are now facing?

Changes

September 2020

So September's here with changes afoot
As students return for their lessons
Adults are encouraged to go back to work
Where employers are not going to question

Has it gone?

October 2020

Just when
We thought it'd waned
It's back with a vengeance
And now a new lockdown begins
Stay safe

Mini lockdown

November 2020

Okay
Lockdown kicks in
on fifth of November
When will this virus go away?
We pray

What about Christmas?

So Christmas could be cancelled
As new cases are going up
But in Tier 3, it seems to be
We'll be ok with luck
But no, with just three days to go
Tier 4 became our fate
Lockdown for us is a heavy blow
When will this "thing" abate?

New Year - New beginnings

Dec 2020

So, as we ring out the end of a year
Which saw much sorrow and pain
Let's pray that soon we'll be free of this scourge
And we can get back to our normal again

Vaccines are rolled out to one and all
And tougher restrictions are clear
We all need to keep safe, take care, stay in
So we can ring in a healthy, Covid free year

CHAPTER 10 - LATTER YEARS

Home

My home is my happy place
And filled with lots of fun
A welcome at my door step
To all and everyone

It's a sanctuary, a comfort
My confidante, my rock
A talking, sharing, caring place
A place where to take stock

In my kitchen or my garden
Home always make the space
For family, friends or barbecues
And six grandkids to touch base

Silence in nature

My soul steers me into nature's near silence
Hearing only the quiet birdsong
And the gentle whisper of the hedgerows
Spurring me to wander further along

Try, try and try again.

If at first you don't succeed,
Try, try and try again
Words my father taught me
As I was growing up
And I took his words to heart
I hadn't done well at school you see
So I took classes in shorthand
And typing too
And hey it was great - as I jolly
Well passed them all - woohoo!

This gave me the option when
I started work to make my dad proud
And prove I was secretarial fodder
This I did and my career became profound

Many years later after raising my children
I finally had the chance to fulfil
A dream I'd had to raise the bar
And study for a degree of my own free will

So at sixty years old I started my journey
Which took six long years of hard work
Reading - Humanities and Classical Studies
Long essays, exams, reading could not be shirked

I am pleased to say how very proud
I was at my Uni graduation
I was presented with my BA Honours degree
With my family to enjoy my elation

If at first you don't succeed ….

People watching

I often like to people watch
As they go about their day
Shoppers dashing to the stores
The joggers on their way
Commuters rushing for the train
Before the whistle blows
Parents on the school run
Before the gates are closed
Youngsters with their heads down
Looking at their phones
Bumping into everyone
Causing lots of moans and groans
Eavesdropping snips of gossip
Quarrels sometimes taking place
Sadness, anger, happiness
Reflected in the face
An eclectic mix of ages
Of people passing me
You might well think I'm nosey
No - just ever so slightly intrigued

Early walk

An early walk for me today
Before the morning heat
AirPods in and off I strolled
To walk the empty streets

The lanes I usually head for
Were very much out of the way
Too remote for me alone
I can go there another day

So around the block it was for me
As the households began their day
The smell of bacon and sausages
And fresh coffee all came my way
As well as perfume and sprays
And some nice aftershaves as well
My walk was definitely different today
And it heightened my sense of smell

A sanctuary

A few days away at a country hotel
It was just where we needed to go
It was a haven, a sanctuary a perfect location
And a place of quiet repose

We could almost forget the months of restrictions
As we lounged by the swimming pool
Cloud spotting, people watching, reading too
And dipping to keep us cool

Benfleet

I now live in a town called Benfleet
In the district of castle point
Thirty miles east of London
A great city to be enjoyed

Several churches and many a pub
Shops in all shapes and sizes
Castle point leisure is just up the road
And three libraries, now there's a surprise

A battle of Benfleet once took place
Between the Vikings and Anglo Saxons
The year was 894 AD
The Danes were defeated by our actions
We have a link to Henry Vlll
With a 13th century castle at Hadleigh park
He used to visit back in the day
But now the remains are quite stark

So, I live next door to the local manor
Where Henry was often a guest
A priests' hole linked to the local church
to hide the clergy from being oppressed

I moved to the area forty plus years ago
And its been very sublime
I'd moved from an island in the Thames
More on that another time….

Books

Books are very tactile and
I have to have a smell
As I open it from new

Then I look at the back
To see what people say
And get their point of view

Then I fan out the pages
As they're often compressed
then read the book I shall pursue

Garden

We love our garden all year long
We've robins and squirrels and a fox or two
A summerhouse and gazebo to relax
And not forgetting the barbecue

I have to confess I do like to plan
I know how I like it and where things should go
But its him indoors who does the hard graft
Mowing and pruning and making things grow

At the end of the day when all's said and done
We make a good gardening pair
Shovels and pruners are packed away
And now a bottle of 'Pinot' to share!

Clouds

Cloud spotting calms me
I see them drift into shapes.
Only known to me

Morning has broken

There's nothing like the silence of an early morning
When others are in their beds
A time for mindfulness and calm
When quiet reflections enter my head
Soon Robins and blackbirds start their trilling
The bees are buzzing, the toads are croaking
The butterflies floating quietly by
Another day's Morning has broken.

Ageing?

The years have flown and before I knew it
I'm of an age I knew would come
Growing older is a natural stage
But in my head I still feel young !?

The aches and pains have now kicked in
hips and knees, feet and neck
Not forgetting hard of hearing
And glasses to see - flippin heck!

But over the years life has treated me well
I'm happy and content and have my health
A wonderful husband, two fabulous kids
Grandchildren, friends and life itself

One of those days

It was one of those days, you know the kind?
Nothing went right, traffic was bad
Queues everywhere, late for work
Losing patience just a tad

But then I think back to the days of lockdown
When we'd give anything to go outside
So I count my blessings those days have passed
And make the most of each day as it arrives

Hearing nature

I sit on a rickety bench, beneath the oak tree
Dappled sunlight pouring through the leaves
A Robin hopping around the greenery
A chaffinch singing as she flees

The sounds of golfers teeing off
On the fairway across the way
The tree rustling in the gentle breeze
And the squirrels are out to play

I'm sitting here in Belfairs park
On this day of bright blue skies
I can hear the sound of horses 'hooves
Means my grandchildren have finished their ride

I am what I am.

I am what I am
Take me or leave me
I am impatient - very
I am truthful
I am a Christian
I am a writer
I am a trusted loving wife
I am a devoted mother
I am a loving grandma
I am a good friend
I love my family
I enjoy cooking - a lot
I am an optimist
I am empathetic
I am a worrier
I get anxious
I am creative
I am wise
I am happy
I am loved

I am what I am

Piano

I'd love to play the piano
But I only play by ear
I cannot read the music
So I don't because of fear
I play a tune with my right hand
But chords I get in a muddle
My left hand gets tied up in knots
And all I do is Fumble

Mirror

Mirror mirror on the wall
Who is that person looking at me
You do me no justice at all today
I look like ninety three

To be fair my hair is a mess
My makeup has almost faded
My fringe needs trimming
And I'm looking pretty jaded
The mirror never lies they say
But it can be fooled
So after my trip to the spa today
My 'before 'and 'after' are pretty cool

The island

The island I lived on as I was growing up
Lies below the sea level of the Thames
There are Dutch connections from the 1600s
they came to look at the drainage and mend

They built sea walls to stop overflowing tides
from flooding salt marshes and more
They put in dykes to drain away water
From roads, in case of a tidal bore

There are signs of their past presence
To this very day - street names and much more
Cornelius Vermuyden was the man in charge
And a school is thus named in his honour

Driving

When I was nineteen back in the day
I started to learn to drive
I failed the test miserably
But yay passed the second - high five!

So I bought myself a little car
That was well within my means
It was an "old banger" a Ford Popular
And so old it was falling apart at the seams
I drove it nervously to begin with
Not very far I have to say
It rattled, squeaked, choked and coughed
And it was soon very obvious it'd had its day

Trivial over thinker

I am an over thinker
about the most trivial things
day by day
like time, the lack of it
and how quickly it flies
what might people think of me
and what I do
am I dressed for the
right occasion
should I do this or that
worried if I've hurt someone or
inadvertently done something wrong
the weather
the traffic
parking spaces, will there be any?
and so it goes on
but for what it's worth
I'll probably never change
accept me for who I am
I'm an over thinker

Lean on me

Lean on me when you're feeling down
I've got a listening ear
It's good to talk and share your woes
And you know I'm always here
Lean on me when things get tough
And all you want is to talk and share
I may not know the answers
But trust me I'll be there

Love at first sight?

I knew straight away
He did too from the start
I'd get butterflies
And I had a racing heart

It was March 1969
In the New Moon
He'd been watching me
Smiling from across the room

It didn't take long to start going steady
We had a connection straight away
We loved each other, that's for sure
From our meeting that very first day

Our wedding

After an 18 month whirlwind romance we said our "I do's" on Sunday 4th October 1970 at 12.30. Our wedding reception was held in a local hall and we hired a team of caterers for our wedding breakfast. We danced the afternoon away to the music of a three piece band and left for our honeymoon about 5pm.

We didn't have a car back then so we were given a lift to the train station by Uncle Jack who had to stop on the way to buy something? When we arrived at the station nearly all of the guests were waiting on the platform to give us a send off. Uncle Jack's ploy paid off. When we boarded the train, the guard locked us in! It was a fabulous send off with "just married" written all over the glass in lipstick.

Arriving at our hotel the receptionist asked if we were newly weds.
So there's me in a large hat, John still wearing his buttonhole, and bits of confetti still on our clothes! "No" we said "what makes you think that?!!"

If they hadn't guessed by then they certainly would have the next day because when I unpacked, tons of confetti fell out of a jumper which my naughty mum had planted inside and hence covered the carpet.

Lots of memories of our wedding to pass down to the next generations.

Our Children

Apart from my Husband, our children Emma and Jonathan are the best thing that has ever happened to me. They are my moon and stars and I love them to bits. Fun loving and reckless as children; as adults they are now happy go lucky achievers who enjoy challenges and fun filled lives. They have given me such joy and pride. The lights of my life.

Golden Wedding Anniversary

So October's here, my favourite month
When memories begin to unfold
Of days gone by and the journey we took
To reach this year of our "gold"

Fifty years ago I said "I do"
To you the love of my life
We celebrate on the 4th of this month
Of the day I became your wife.

Five decades have flown by
Those years have simply gone
We worked and saved and bought our house
And our two special children came along

Ups and downs - we've had them
Redundancies, struggles and strife
But at the end of the day we've alway been happy
And our love continues for life

We've travelled afar and had such fun
With friends and families too
Encountered capers and many adventures
In seaplanes, 'copters, and balloons
So, grandparents we have now become
Six - we've been wonderfully blessed
They give us such pleasure and lots of love
And completed our family nest

*I believed
I could
so I did*

Milton Keynes UK
Ingram Content Group UK Ltd.
UKHW011032250424
441751UK00001B/33